G-4244
$6.95

THE COURAGE TO SAY NO

Twenty-three Songs
for Lent and Easter

John L. Bell
&
Graham Maule

The Iona Community

A complete recording is available from the publisher.
Compact Disc   CD-369
Cassette   CS-369

GIA Publications, Inc.
Chicago

First Published in 1996

The Wild Goose is a Celtic symbol of the Holy Spirit.
It is the trademark of Iona Community Publications

© 1996 Iona Community/ Wild Goose Resource Group
Published and distributed in North America exclusively by GIA Publications, Inc.
ISBN: 0-941050-84-X

GIA Publications, Inc,
7404 S. Mason Ave.
Chicago, IL 60638
U.S.A.
(708) 496-3800

CONTENTS

INTRODUCTION

Two years ago we published a collection of songs for Advent and Christmas entitled *Innkeepers and Light Sleepers*. Those were both for congregational and choral use and have gained wide acceptance.

We were therefore encouraged to look at the possibility of a similar collection dealing with the seasons of Lent and Easter. This book is the result. It has some similarities with the previous publication. For example, the songs do not attach themselves simply to the high point of the season, but are spread out from Ash Wednesday to the Sunday after the Ascension. Too often, Christmas Day and Easter Day benefit from the attention of song writers, but the journey to and from these Holy Days is less well-served with words and music.

Another similarity is that nearly all the songs are arranged in four-part harmony which should be within the reach and compass of most choirs. This is not a selection of test pieces to show the dexterity of the performers. It is an assortment of songs which should be satisfying for choirs and music groups to sing and yet provides material which is also accessible to congregations.

But there are also dissimilarities.

Innkeepers and Light Sleepers has several songs which may be accompanied on guitar. *The Courage to Say No* has fewer. This is not out of spite to either the instrument or its exponents, but simply because in many songs the harmony changes so quickly that strummed accompaniment would be well nigh impossible. Similarly, there are several songs which, having folk-tune melodies, should not be accompanied by keyboard. A mature and sensitive church musician will discern when to accompany and what to use; a lazy church musician will presume that nothing is possible unless he or she is providing instrumental backing. For countless centuries all that accompanied the human voice was percussion. People's vocal confidence—contrary to presumed wisdom—actually increases when they are occasionally enabled to sing *a cappella*.

Another innovation in this collection is the incorporation of songs which come from African and African-American traditions. Our two volumes of World Church Songs, *Many and Great* and *Sent by the Lord*, have opened up for many the rich treasuries of song accessible to us in the repertoire of the churches of the Southern Hemisphere. But if we are really to take such music seriously, it should not simply be published in volumes separate from items of European origin. Here we are glad to incorporate material from Ethiopia, Tanzania, Ghana and Malawi as well as two traditional spirituals.

Few of these songs are contemporary with the publication of the book. The vast majority have been sung, scrutinised and amended several times in the past five or six years and have proven their worth in places far from a printing press.

May Christ, whose ultimate journey they celebrate, use them to God's glory and for the nourishment of God's people.

John L. Bell

Songs
for Lent

The courage to say No

Tune: COURAGE TO SAY NO (JLB)

Quietly and Slowly

1. When Sa - tan speaks in an - gel tones and
2. When stones to bread means more for us, and
3. When climb - ing high at - tracts a crowd and
4. When bow - ing down to serve the worst brings
5. When Sa - tan speaks in an - gel tones and

sanc - ti - fies the road to ru - in;
more for us seems most al - lur - ing;
cheap ac - claim per - verts our call - ing; if on that path we're
all we want but breaks our con - science;
sanc - ti - fies the road to ru - in;

The stories of how Jesus was tempted in the wilderness, stories we associate closely with the season of Lent, are very unique. They could only have come from the mouth of Jesus, as no-one else was present to witness what was happening. Their relevance for today becomes apparent when we recognise that Jesus was asked to do things which, to all intents and purposes, seemed right, but for the worst possible motives.

Some poignancy is added to this song if it is sung by three different voices, from different parts of the same building, roughly representing the different venues in which the temptations took place, as well as the different voices of the tempter. The first singer should take verses 1, 2 & 5 and may find it most effective to sing 5 completely unaccompanied, or have the accompaniment fade out mid–verse.

Have mercy upon me, O God

Tune: MISERERE ME (JLB)

Psalm 51

Steadily

1. Have mer-cy up-on me, O God, ac - cor - ding to your lov-ing kind-ness;

wash from me all my in - i - qui-ty; cleanse me from my sin.

2. Well I know the wrong I've done; my sin is al-ways be - fore me. A -

gainst you on-ly I have sinned and done what is e - vil.

3. You de - sire faith - ful-ness with - in, so teach me wis-dom in my

heart; purge me and wash me tru - ly clean, make me whit - er than snow.

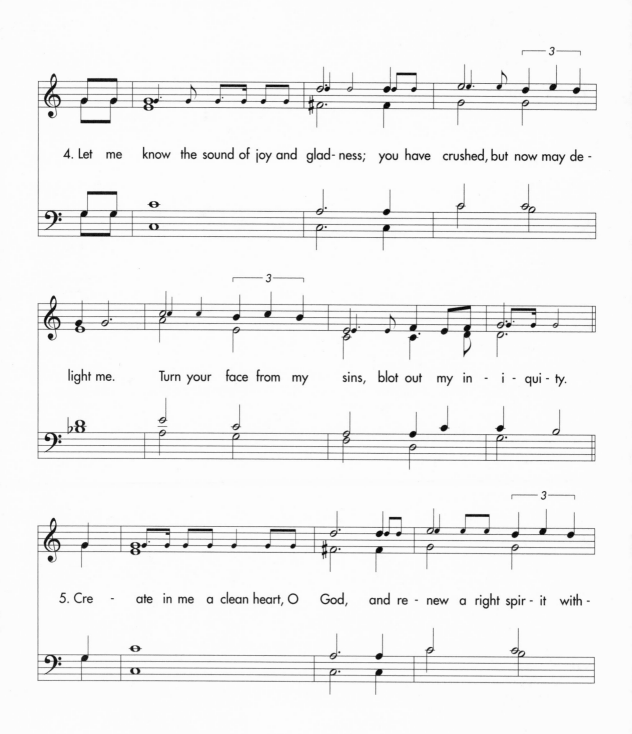

4. Let me know the sound of joy and glad-ness; you have crushed, but now may de-

light me. Turn your face from my sins, blot out my in - i - qui - ty.

5. Cre - ate in me a clean heart, O God, and re - new a right spir - it with-

in me; do not drive me out from your pres - ence or take your spir - it from me.

6. My God, de-liv-er me from e - vil and I shall de-clare your sal - va - tion;

Lord, o-pen my lips and my mouth shall pro - claim your praise.

This Psalm is set to be sung either by a unison voice with keyboard accompaniment, or four–part harmony or both. If voices are singing in harmony, the under–parts simply replicate the rhythm indicated by the small notes of the soprano line.

Love which understands

Tune: BANCHORY (JLB)

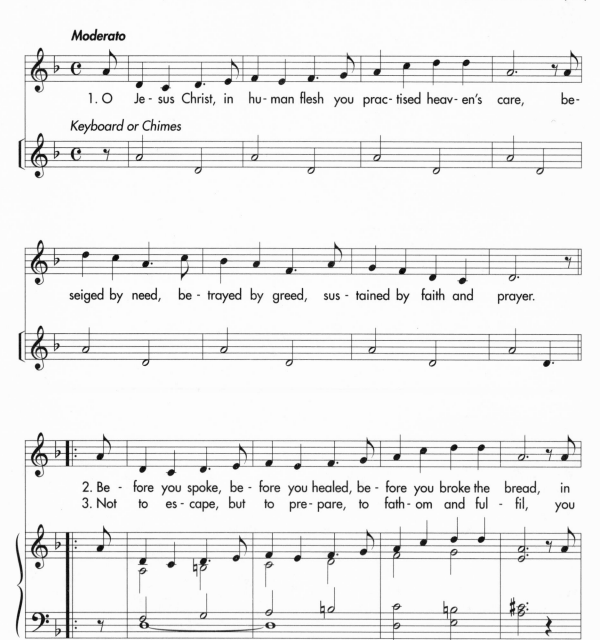

Moderato

1. O Je - sus Christ, in hu - man flesh you prac - tised heav - en's care, be-

Keyboard or Chimes

seiged by need, be - trayed by greed, sus - tained by faith and prayer.

2. Be - fore you spoke, be - fore you healed, be - fore you broke the bread, in
3. Not to es - cape, but to pre - pare, to fath - om and ful - fil, you

crowds, as in the qui - et place, you felt for where God led.
let your heart and hands be tuned, in si - lence, to God's will.

Women

4. So we, re- spond - ing to your call to walk your cho - sen way, ad -

Men

4. So we, re- spond- ing to your call to walk your cho - sen

Keyboard or Chimes

mit our need to learn from you to love and work and pray.

way, ad - mit our need to learn from you to love and work and pray.

5. Then send your Spir - it to in- spire our cau- tious hearts and hands, till

work and prayer are root- ed deep in love which un - der - stands.

The temptations are but one of a sequence of Gospel stories which indicate that, for Jesus, caring was not just a matter of doing, but also a matter of preparing through prayer and reflection. He frequently went to a quiet place to escape the crowds; he encouraged his disciples to emulate his practice; and their failure to do that resulted in their inability to stay watching and praying with him in Gethsemane.

This is essentially a unison song. It may be sung solo unaccompanied, as a duet, or with a choir and congregation. In event of the last option, the following is suggested:

> v1 Solo voice (with chimes or keyboard)
> 2 Women
> 3 Men
> 4 Choir singing in canon
> 5 All

There are a number of other suitable Common metre tunes, such as *This Endrys Night, St. Columba* and *Gerontius* which can be used as alternatives.

Travelling the road to freedom

Tune: TRAVELLING (JLB)

frenzied people, puzzled by what they
faith and patience, neither of which is
yet forgiving, ev'n when my friends most
izing evil only a traveller

hear and see: travelling the road to freedom,
plain to see: travelling the road to freedom,
disagree: travelling the road to freedom,
can repair. Travelling the road to freedom,

who wants to travel the road with me?
who wants to travel the road with me?
who wants to travel the road with me?
I am the Way, I'll take you there.

The engagement of people in celebrating the season of Lent is often spoken of in terms of a journey.
And this is perfectly appropriate, because the intention of Jesus was never to sit still like a guru in
a retreat house and have people come and bow at his feet. Rather, he summoned people to follow
behind him, and in Lent we are challenged to review how closely we are following, and how far
we have moved in our discipleship.

This is a very simple AABA tune which can be sung in unison, but is more effective when
harmonised. It may be used as a recessional during Lent and has evident associations with Holy
Week.

Where a choir has insufficient altos for the two lines, *either* sing one alto line, beginning on the F in
bars 1, 9, 25, moving to the Eb in the subsequent bars and singing the lower part thereafter; *or*
have a light tenor sing the lower part throughout.

Lay down your head

Tune: RESTING (JLB)

1. Lay down your head, Lord Je - sus Christ, fast falls the night. Close fol - low those who crave your end, blind - ed by sight. God give you rest,
2. All that you've done and all you've said, suf - fered, and shared, proves you're the one for whom the world waits un - pre - pared. Had you con - formed,
3. What lies a - head we fear to guess, you fail to fear: hopes seem to fade, heaven seems far, hell seems so near. Here, with our faith
4. Lay down your head, Lord Je - sus Christ, fast falls the night. Close fol - low those who crave your end, blind - ed by sight. God give you rest,

strength for your task,   light for our way.   Lay down your head
had   you con-doned,   had you comp-lied,   none would be heard
stretched to the full,   put to the test,   you calm-ly talk,
strength for your task,   light for our way.   Lay down your head

and,   by your side,   we'll   sleep and   stay.
pric - ing your head,   nurs - ing their   pride.
then   kneel to pray,   then   take your   rest.
and,   by your side,   we'll   sleep and   stay.

It is normally at Christmas, in carols such as *Little Jesus, sweetly sleep*, that we express that kind of close and tender intimacy with Jesus which the Gospels show him clearly expressing to his friends. Often we sing about Christ, but in this song, which is a kind of Lenten evening carol, we sing directly to him.

If at all possible, the song should be sung in harmony and unaccompanied. It has been frequently proven that if a choir or music group sing the first three verses, the congregation, without any rehearsal, can easily join in the final verse.

Oh freedom

Proudly

Tune: African-American Traditional (arr. by JLB)

1. Oh_____ free - dom! Oh_____ free - dom! Oh_____ free-dom o - ver me.
2. No mo' moan - in', no mo' moan - in', moan - in', no mo' moan - in' o - ver me.
3. No mo' weep - in', no mo' weep - in', weep - in', no mo' weep - in' o - ver me.
4. There'll be sing - in', there'll be sing - in', sing - in', there'll be sing - in' o - ver me.
5. There'll be shout - in', there'll be shout - in', shout - in', there'll be shout - in' o - ver me.
6. There'll be pray - in', there'll be pray - in', pray - in', there'll be pray - in' o - ver me.

This is one of a number of songs coming from black cultures. *Oh Freedom!* is reckoned to be one of the earliest spirituals whose origins might well have been in the song of West Africa. The words, which have a hint of the ambiguity embedded in many similar spirituals, are pertinent to Jesus who fulfilled completely the sentiment of the text. Rather than be a slave to sin or Satan, he was crucified, dead and buried. In his death and resurrection, he put an end to the fear of death and rooted Christian worship thereafter in joyful song and prayer.

Opinions as to how the text should be sung vary – as might be expected with music which is essentially in a folk idiom. However three guidelines have held the consensus of several black spiritual singers:

a) A regular rhythm, as expected of a working song, should be present throughout. White choirs, especially in Great Britain, have a tendency to sentimentalise the spirituals by unnecessary and endless rubato.

b) If this were in French, singers would attempt the pronunciation as nearly as they could approximate to the original. Similarly with spirituals, the integrity of the song is respected when the pronunciation of the words, as far as possible, replicates that of native singers. This means that words such as "mo'" should be left without a consonant to end the vowel sound.

c) Normal European practice aims at producing long vowel sounds, with the consonants as precise and clipped as possible. This should not apply to spirituals where an 'm' or 'n' sound is concerned. In other words such as "moanin'" the second vowel should be short and the final consonant should resonate through the singer's head and lips.

Arrangement © 1996 WGRG, The Iona Community. GIA Publications, exclusive North American Agent.

Songs
for Passiontide

Sing, my soul

Tune: MYSIE (JLB)

Gently

1. Sing, my soul, when hope is sleep - ing, sing when faith gives way to fears; sing to melt the ice of sad - ness, mak - ing way for joy through tears.

2. Sing, my soul, when sick - ness lin - gers, sing to dull the sharp - est pain; sing to set the spir - it leap - ing: heal - ing needs a glad re - frain.

3. Sing, my soul, of him who shaped me, let me wan - der far a - way, ran with o - pen arms to greet me, brought me home a - gain to stay.

4. Sing, my soul, when light seems dark - est, sing when night re - fus - es rest, sing though death should mock the fu - ture: what's to come by God is blessed.

This essentially solo song is a paraphrase of a letter from an elderly saintly woman whose testimony is that, even in her lowest days, when she speaks to God he listens, and then she sings to rejoice both her heart and his. It is well suited to the Saturday of Holy Week or to other occasions when loss or weakness are evident.

Behold the Holy Lamb of God

Tumbuka hymn (Malawi)
by Charles Chinula
Trans. by Helen Taylor
Adapt. by Tom Colvin
Tune: HOLY LAMB (arr. JLB)

In stately fashion

1. Be - hold the ho - ly Lamb of God,
2. In si - lent grief and dig - ni - ty;
3. And there, out - side the cit - y wall,
4. But lis - ten to his heart - felt cry,
5. Ye - su, while dy - ing on that tree,

Ye
he
high
"My
for -

su, the one who lifts for us a heav - y load.
takes the cross and walks that way to set us free.
on the cross they nail the one who saves us all.
God, my God, now will you leave me here to die?"
gives our fol - ly and our sins and sets us free.

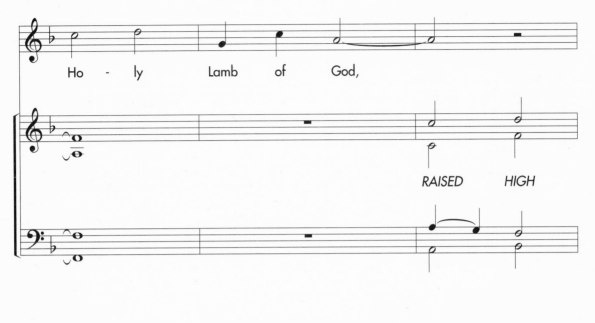

Ho - ly   Lamb   of   God,

RAISED   HIGH

ON   THE   CROSS   TO   BEAR   FOR   US   THE   PAIN AND LOSS.

This simple but magnificent song of the passion comes from Malawi. This arragement was made from a very basic transcription which indicated the dialogical nature of the song.

It is particularly effective when used to accompany the procession of the cross into a community gathered for worship on Good Friday. As with other songs from Africa, it can be sung with a cantor and congregation, in unison, or as harmonised above.

Words (in Chi Tumbuka, Malawi) and music by the Rev. Charles Chinula (1885-1970). Translated by Miss Helen Taylor, adapted by Tom Colvin. Words and Music © 1995 by Hope Publishing Co., Carol Stream, IL 60188. All rights reserved. Used by permission.

When the Son of God was dying

Tune: GOLGOTHA (JLB)

Steadily

1. When the Son of God was dy - ing, long a -
2. Crowds which once had cried, "Ho - san - na!" lost their
3. Hor - ror, hurt, and pain found home in Mar - y's
4. Hu - man - kind re - peats Gol - go - tha ev - ery
5. Je - sus, lay your bod - y in this sad earth's

go, some played dice and some knelt cry - ing,
voice: hell had grinned to hear Ba - rab - bas
breast, watch - ing tor - ture's toll and hear - ing
day: God gets gagged while friends and fol - lowers
grave; on - ly one who suf - fers can pre -

lost and low. Cyn - ics sneered and
was their choice; Ju - das hung him -
sol - diers jest. Where was God to
turn a - way. Prof - it threat - ens
sume to save. End hy - poc - ri -

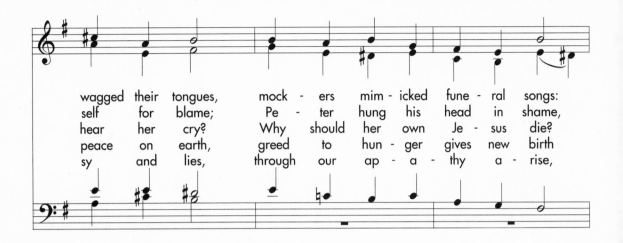

wagged their tongues, mock- ers mim- icked fune- ral songs:
self for blame; Pe- ter hung his head in shame,
hear her cry? Why should her own Je- sus die?
peace on earth, greed to hun- ger gives new birth
sy and lies, through our ap- a- thy a- rise,

this, while God's own Son was dy- ing, long a- go.
while the crowds which cried, "Ho- san- na!" lost their voice.
Grief and ag- o- ny found home in Mar- y's breast.
as the world re- peats Gol- go- tha ev- ery day.
bring us the sal- va- tion which our spir- its crave.

There is a sense in which all the classic hymns of the cross – be they chorales like *O Sacred Head* or spirituals like *Were You There?* – tell the story and little more. Good Friday is not really the time to theologise or work out doctrines of the atonement. It is the time when we recognise, in the people around the cross, something of ourselves; and when we realise that, despite the centuries which intervene, the world still exhibits an uncanny ability to recrucify Christ in the personal and corporate failures to do justly, love mercy and walk humbly with God.

When finest aspirations fail

Tune: APRIL 9th (JLB)

Sadly

1. When fin-est as-pir-a-tions fail and dreams be-come dis-may, and
2. We hurt for what has hap-penedand we fear for what's to come; and
3. Shall they con-trol our des-tin-y who, deaf to our de-mands, are
4. Oh Christ, you lost con-trol, or so it seems, when to a tree they
5. Then must our hopes, like you, be bro-ken down be-yond re-pair; must
6. And shall our hopes, like you, a-rise from where they ceased to be; and

all the hopes to-mor-row held lie felled by yes-ter-day, what
eas-y con-so-la-tion leaves us neg-a-tive and numb, and
ruled by oth-er val-ues and de-fer to their com-mands?And
nailed you and re-gailed you and re-fused to set you free; and
we be lost and pow-er-less, be-friend-ed by des-pair, in
shall the spir-it that was crushed be trans-formed and set free? If

can we do, where do we turn, what shall we say?
won - d'ring wheth - er deep - er depths are yet to plumb.
are our fu - tures safe in these un - want - ed hands?
all be - cause you showed how life was meant to be.
or - der some - how to be saved and sense God's care?
that's God's will, then we a - wait what's yet to be.

This is a song to be sung after the remembrance of the cruficixion, perhaps on Holy Saturday. It aims to associate all the brokenness which we experience with the brokenness of Christ, in order that, through him and in imitation of him, disintegrated lives may come together again.

This song was first used, not during Holy Week, but after a staggering blow which a community sustained. In view of this, verse 3 is probably best omitted, if the song is being used at Passiontide.

Thank you for the night

Tune: COMPLIMENT (JLB)

Gently

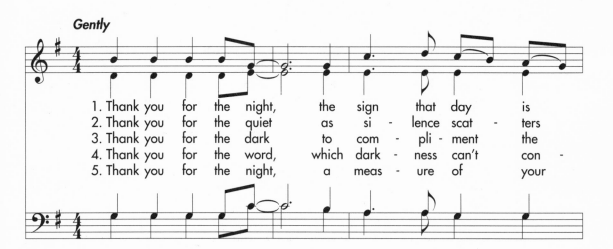

1. Thank you for the night, the sign that day is
2. Thank you for the quiet as si - lence scat - ters
3. Thank you for the dark to com - pli - ment the
4. Thank you for the word, which dark - ness can't con -
5. Thank you for the night, a meas - ure of your

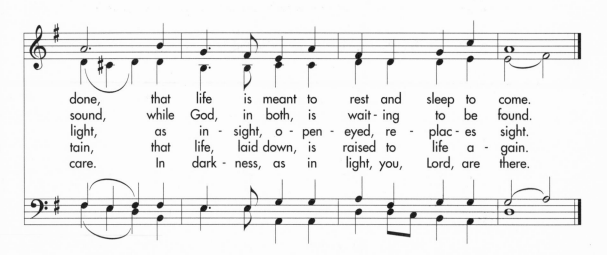

done, that life is meant to rest and sleep to come.
sound, while God, in both, is wait - ing to be found.
light, as in - sight, o - pen - eyed, re - plac - es sight.
tain, that life, laid down, is raised to life a - gain.
care. In dark - ness, as in light, you, Lord, are there.

This gentle vesper may be used at the close of a Good Friday service, or on the eve of Easter, if there is to be no vigil. It is not exclusively for the Easter season, but is most appropriate in this context.

Songs
for Easter

Maranatha!

Tune: MARANATHA (JLB)

1. Word of the Fa - ther,
2. First - born of Mar - y,
3. Heal - er and help - er,
4. Ser - vant and suf - ferer,
5. Je - sus, re - deem - er,
6. Christ, res - sur - rect - ed,
7. Ma - ra - na - tha!

COME, LORD, COME

AND TAKE OUR FEAR A - WAY, AND TAKE OUR FEAR A - WAY;

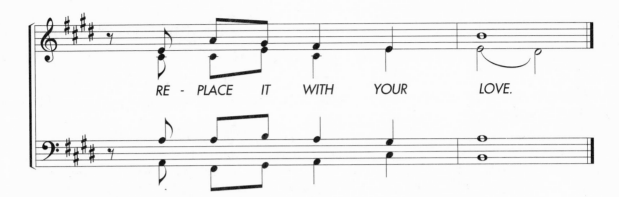

RE - PLACE IT WITH YOUR LOVE.

Maranatha is an ancient Aramaic word which means, "Let our Lord come!" It is a prayerful summons to call God into our midst and may be found in 1st Corinthians Ch.16, v.22.

It is therefore an appropriate word to use during an Easter vigil, as the congregation waits for the announcement of the resurrection. The various titles attributed to Jesus can be added to, or omitted, as the situation requires.

For its best use, the song should be sung just before the announcement of the resurrection is made. The cantor should be at the back of the church, well out of sight. This is a song of communal pleading, not a performance piece.

Jesus is risen, Alleluia!

(Mfurahini, Haleluya - Tanzania)

Text: Bernard Kyamanywa
(trans. by JBL)

Tune: Haya Traditional (arr. by JLB)

Joyfully

1. Je - sus is ris - en, al - le - lu - ia!
2. Bur - ied for three days, des - tined for death,
3. "Don't be a - fraid!" the an - gel had said,
4. "Go and tell oth - ers, Christ is a - live;
5. Christ has a - ris - en! Now all can see
6. Let heav - en ech - o, let the earth sing:

Wor - ship and praise him, al - le - lu - ia!
now he re - turns to breathe with our breath.
"Why seek the liv - ing here with the dead?
love is e - ter - nal, faith and hope thrive.
how hu - man - kind is meant to be free.
Je - sus is sav - iour of ev - ery - thing.

Now our re - deem - er bursts from the grave;
Blest are the ears a - lert to his voice,
Look where he lay, his bod - y is gone,
What God in - tend - ed, Je - sus ful - filled;
Though pow'rs of dark - ness threat - en their worst,
All those who trust him, Christ will re - ceive;

lost to the tomb, Christ ris - es to save.
blest are the hearts which for him re - joice.
ris - en and vi - brant, warm with the sun."
what God con - ceives can ne - ver be killed."
through e - very bar - rier Je - sus has burst.
there - fore re - joice, o - bey and be - lieve!

COME, LET US WOR - SHIP HIM, END - LESS - LY SING;

AL - LE - LU - IA!   AL - LE - LU - IA!

CHRIST IS A - LIVE AND DEATH LOS - ES ITS STING.

AL - LE - LU - IA!   AL - LE - LU - IA!

SINS ARE FOR - GIV - EN, AL - LE - LU - IA!

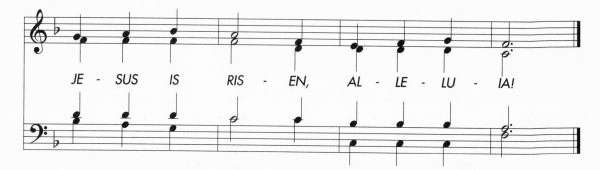

JE - SUS IS RIS - EN, AL - LE - LU - IA!

This bright tune, with its very straightforward AABA form, sits very comfortably on Western lips, despite originating in Central Africa. This song appears in several versions in Europe and the USA. These are invariably Lutheran publications, Lutherans being a significant denomination in Tanzania.

For reasons of clarity and sensibility, this text does not follow previously published versions, but aims to represent the gist of the original. Similarly, as source documents vary immensely in their arrangement of the tune, the above represents a completely new version, though emulating discernible African rhythmic and harmonic practices.

It can be sung as a choral piece, with the congregation joining the chorus; or as a congregational song in its entirety. If the latter is the case, vary the people or groups singing the verses. People engage more with the text when they don't have to sing every word.

Akanamandla

Tune: South African Traditional

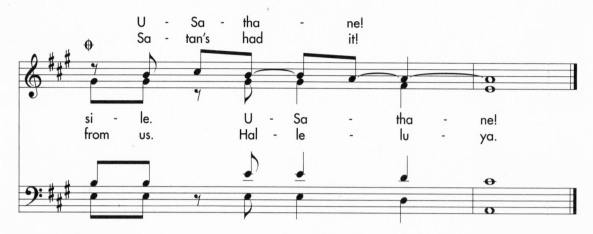

1. Akanamandla,
   Haleluya,
   Akanamandla,
   USathane!

2. Simdumazile,
   Haleluya,
   Simdumazile,
   USathane!

3. Simsabisile,
   Haleluya,
   Simsabisile,
   USathane!

1. He has no power.
   Haleluya.
   He has no power.
   Satan's had it!

2. He has been cheated.
   Haleluya.
   He has been cheated.
   Satan's had it!

3. He flees far from us.
   Haleluya.
   He flees far from us.
   Satan's had it!

Akanamandla was one of the first songs from South Africa which was promoted in Great Britan by the Iona Community in the mid 1980's. It came in a collection, *Freedom Is Coming*, produced by the Swedish Mission Church and at once became popular as a song of both protest and praise. Like the spirituals, it contains an ambiguity. It sings not only of the triumph of Jesus over Satan, but also of the ultimate triumph of freedom over apartheid, a reality eventually celebrated in South Africa in May 1994.

This song was one which, with others, black people sang in the face of persecution and intimidation at funerals, on demonstrations, in churches. Its full Xhosa text is printed here, but most choirs or music groups may prefer to sing only the first verse in the indigenous language, then sing three in English and return to *akanamandla* for the final verse.

The word *akanamandla* has a popular pedigree in songs of praise and protest in the black church in South Africa. It should be remembered and repeated in all other places where the resurrecting power of God, seen first in Christ, is discerned also in public and political life.

Words and music ©1984 Utryck, Uppsala, Sweden, used by permission of Walton Music Corporation.

The Lord of all

Tune: LORD OF ALL (JLB)

At a lively pace

1. The Bread of Life, the car - pen - ter's own son, has made a
2. He is the Al - pha and the O - me - ga, the King of
3. He is the Ser - vant suf - fering for our wrong and yet the
4. Each beat - ing heart, each bod - y and each mind are sum - moned

Dmaj7   Dm7

feast and calls us to his ta - ble. His food is
Love and thus the Prince of Peace. What he be -
Lord who danc - es on the grave. He helps the
still to an - swer to his call. Who - ev - er

Em7   A7   D

ME. SO LET YOUR HANDS MEET MINE AND SHARE THE

BREAD AND WINE THAT SETS US FREE.

THAT SETS US FREE.

This very lively song is ideal for celebrations of the eucharist in the weeks following Easter. Being in verse and chorus form, it is helpful to have either a different section of the choir, or of the congregation (men/women/children), sing a verse, with all joining in the chorus.

Christ has risen

Tune: TRANSFORMATION (JLB)

Gently

1. Christ has ris - en while earth slum - bers, Christ has
2. Christ has ris - en for the peo - ple whom he
3. Christ has ris - en to com - pan - ion for - mer
4. Christ has ris - en and for ev - er lives to

ris - en where hope died, as he said and as he
died to love and save; Christ has ris - en for the
friends who fear the night, sens - ing loss and lim - i -
chal - lenge and to change all whose lives are messed or

prom - ised, as we doubt - ed and de - nied. Let the
wom - en bring - ing flowers to grace his grave. Christ has
ta - tion where their faith had once burned bright. They be -
man - gled, all who find re - li - gion strange. Christ is

C   Gm   Gm⁷   C

moon em - brace the bless - ing; let the sun sus - tain the
ris - en for dis - ci - ples hud - dled in an up - stairs
moan what is no long - er, they ex - pect no hope - ful
ris - en, Christ is pres - ent, mak - ing us what he has

Gm/B♭   F/A   E♭/G   Gm⁷

cheer; let the world con - firm the ru - mour: Christ is
room. He whose word in - spired cre - a - tion can't be
sign till Christ ends their con - ver - sa - tion, break - ing
been— ev - i - dence of trans - for - ma - tion in which

C   Gm   Am⁷   B♭

43

ris - en,   God   is   here!
si - lenced   by   the   tomb.
bread and   shar - ing   wine.
God is   known   and   seen.

This is a much gentler Easter song, appropriate for either evening time or for when there is no call for excessive euphoria. This might be the case, for instance, if a death or disaster during Holy Week has stunned a community.

It can be sung solo or by the congregation. In the former case, it might be good to have three different voices taking the first three verses and having either the first voice, or the congregation, sing verse 4.

Easter evening

Tune: THE SILKIE
Scottish Traditional (arr. JLB)

Gently

1. As we walked home at close of day, a stran - ger joined us on our way. He heard us speak of one who'd gone and

2. "Why wan - der fur - ther with - out light? Please stay with us this trou - bled night. We've shared the truth of how we feel and

3. We sat to eat our sim - ple spread, then watched the stran - ger take the bread; and, as he said the bless - ing prayer, we

4. No stran - ger he; it was our eyes which failed to see, in stran - ger's guise, the Lord who, ris - en from the dead, met

5. Al - le - lu - ia! Al - le - lu - ia! Al - le - lu - ia! Al - le - lu - ia! As Mar - y and our sis - ters said, the

45

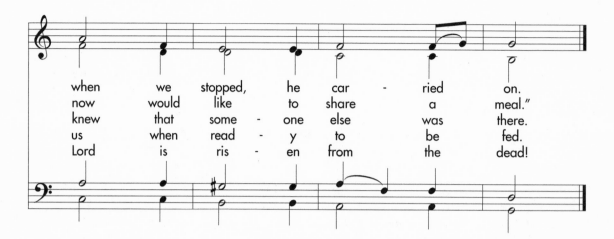

when	we	stopped,	he	car	-	ried	on.
now	would	like	to	share		a	meal."
knew	that	some	- one	else		was	there.
us	when	read	- y	to		be	fed.
Lord	is	ris	- en	from		the	dead!

This is a second, quieter song, for Easter Day and is particularly appropriate at evening, when the Emmaus road story is recounted.

The tune is probably Orcadian in origin and has a beautiful haunting feel about it, which well matches the words. It is essentially a choral song and, as such, is best sung thus:
  v1 solo voice(s) unaccompanied
  2 solo voice(s) singing text with harmony hummed.
  3 harmony sung
  4 harmony sung
  5 unison for first two lines, harmony for last two.

Songs
for the
Post-Easter Period

Tom's song

Tune: LEIS AN LURGHAINN
Scots Gaelic Traditional (arr. JLB)

Steadily

1. Where they

Oh ... Oh ... Oh ... Oh

Oh ... Oh ... Oh ... Oh

(1.) were, I'd have been; what they saw, I'd have seen; what they
(2.) made my de - mand that un - less, at first hand, I could
(3.) tales I called lies till his gaze met my eyes, and the
(4.) stam - mered, "My Lord!" he re - plied with the word, "Those who
(5.) me, ask for proof, sit and sneer, stand a - loof; but be -

Oh ... Oh ... Oh ... Oh

Oh ... Oh ... Oh ... Oh

felt, I'd have shown if I knew what they'd known.
prove what they said, I'd pre - sume he was dead.
words I'd re - hearsed lost their force and dis - persed.
live in God's light walk by faith, not by sight."
lief which is blessed rests on God, not a test.

Oh ... Oh ... Oh ... Oh

Oh ... Oh ... Oh

"PEACE BE WITH YOU," HE SAID, "TAKE MY

HAND, SEE MY SIDE. STOP YOUR DOUBT - ING, BE -

2. So   I
3. All   their
4. When   I
5. Some,   like

Fine   *D.S.*

LIEVE   AND GOD'S   SPIR - IT RE - CEIVE."

Oh

A folk tune conveys the words of this song for the post–Easter period. The words attempt to express the confused and embarrassed condition of Thomas, who was not present when Jesus first showed himself to the apostles after the resurrection. The nature of the tune allows for the melody of the verses, if sung solo, to falter and stumble as the text suggests.

Leis an Lurghainn is usually sung at a brisk pace. However a slower tempo is required for this song. The harmonising parts should endeavour to make their accompaniment during the verses as inobtrusive as possible. Some may prefer to sing "Wo" rather than "Oh", if a slightly more mysterious atmosphere is desired.

You hear the lambs a-cryin'

Tune: African-Caribbean Traditional (arr. JLB)

Slowly

YOU HEAR THE LAMBS A - CRY-IN', HEAR THE LAMBS A -

CRY-IN', HEAR THE LAMBS A - CRY-IN'; O SHEP-HERD, FEED MY SHEEP.

1. My Sav - iour spoke these words so sweet,
2. O Lord, my love you see and know;
3. O was - n't it an aw - ful shame?

hum

Spirituals, as mentioned previously, are work songs. Because of the tender nature of these words, there may be a tendency to sentimentalise, by singing in very hushed tones or making use of rubato. Both tendencies should be avoided. The song can be sung quietly, but it should also communicate the strength, both of faith and of Jesus.

What wondrous love is this

Tune: WONDROUS LOVE (U.S.A.)
Southern Harmony , 1835 (arr. JLB)

1. What won-drous love is this, O my soul, O my
2. To God and to the Lamb I will sing, I will
3. And when from death I'm free, I'll sing on, I'll sing

soul! What won-drous love is this, O my soul! What
sing; to God and to the Lamb I will sing. To
on; and when from death I'm free, I'll sing on. And

What won-drous love is this, O my soul! What
To God and to the Lamb I will sing. To
And when from death I'm free, I'll sing on. And

What won-drous love is this, O my soul! What
To God and to the Lamb I will sing. To
And when from death I'm free, I'll sing on. And

What won - drous love is this, that
To God and to the Lamb___
And when from death I'm free,___

(for rehearsal)

won - drous love is this, that caused the Lord of bliss to
God and to the Lamb, who is the great I Am, while
when from death I'm free, I'll sing and joy - ful be; and

won - drous love is this, that caused the Lord of bliss to
God and to the Lamb, who is the great I Am, while
when from death I'm free, I'll sing and joy - ful be; and

won - drous love is this, that caused the Lord, the Lord of bliss to
God and to the Lamb, who is the great I Am, I Am, while
when from death I'm free, I'll sing and joy - ful, joy - ful be; and

caused the Lord of bliss to lay a -
I will sing while
when from death I'm free, I'm free,

lay a - side his crown for my soul, for my
mil - lions join the theme, I will sing, I will
through e - ter - ni - ty I'll sing on, I'll sing

lay a - side his crown
mil - lions join the theme,
through e - ter - ni - ty

lay, to lay a - side his crown
mil - lions, mil - lions join the theme,
through, and through e - ter - ni - ty

side his crown
mil - lions join,
I'll sing on,

This beautiful American folk hymn has a tune which is firmly in the Dorian mode, suggesting a possible historical link with Scotland.

The four-part harmony setting may be used throughout, though a more fulfilling rendering could involve a solo voice for the 1st verse, harmony for the second, and unison for the third.

When Jesus Christ worked here on earth

Tune: Almaz Belihu (Ethiopia)
Yemissrach Dimts Literature Program

Howard S. Olson (Alt. JLB)

Joyfully

1. When Je - sus Christ worked here on earth, he preached in his home town.
1. M - ji - ni kwa - ke Na - za - ret' ka - se - ma Ye - su wa - zi.
2. The el - ders of the syn - a - gogue were shocked by Ma - ry's son,
2. Wa - zee wa - li - sha - nga - zwa tu na ma - hu - bi - ri va - ke
3. The way he lived was proof of it: he qui - et - ed all strife.
4. So pass it on to - day, my friends, the mes - sage is the same:

I - sa - iah's hopes were now ful - filled, those claims of great re - nown:
Ya ku - wa kwa - ke u - na - bii. wa ka - le u - me - ti - mi - zwa.
that he was des - tined to be - come the Christ for ev - ery - one,
Hu - e - nda hu - yu ni na - bii, na ha - ta Kri - sto Ma - si - hi.
The cross it - self he could not flee, ev'n though it cost his life.
de - liv - er - ance is Christ's to give. For this to earth he came.

Refrain

TO BRING GOOD NEWS TO NEED - Y FOLK, TO HELP THE BLIND TO
KU - SA - I - DI - A MA - SKI - NI, VI - PO - FU NA - O WA -

SEE, TO HEAL THE BRO - KEN HEARTS A - GAIN AND
O - NE. WA - FU - NGWA WA - WE HU - RU TU WA -

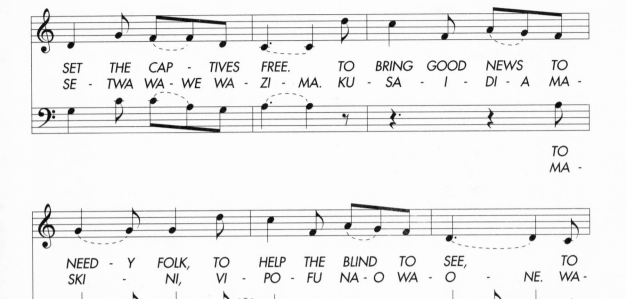

African religious songs frequently do what European songs don't – they tell the story of biblical people and are thus both educational and evangelical.

This song comes from Ethiopia and appeared in the Northern Hemisphere translated by Howard S. Olson in a collection entitled SET FREE, published by Ausburg Fortress, Minneapolis.

Music: Yemissrach Dimts Literature Program, Ethiopia
Words: Howard S. Olson
© 1993, Howard S. Olson

When our master Jesus went away

A teaching song by Tom Colvin
for the Church at Nyohene, Ghana

Tune: NYOHENE
Ghanian Traditional (arr. JLB)

Gently but brightly

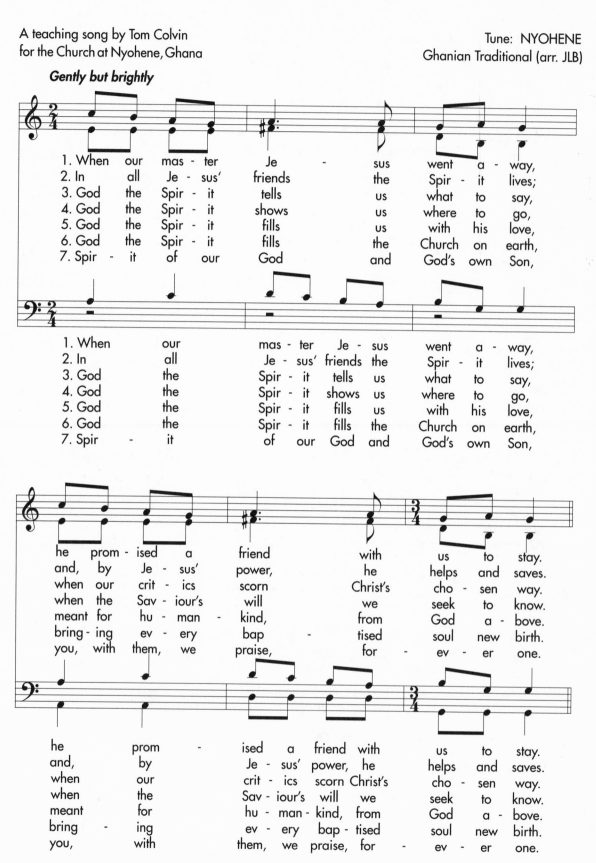

1. When our mas - ter Je - sus went a - way,
2. In all Je - sus' friends the Spir - it lives;
3. God the Spir - it tells us what to say,
4. God the Spir - it shows us where to go,
5. God the Spir - it fills us with his love,
6. God the Spir - it fills the Church on earth,
7. Spir - it of our God and God's own Son,

he prom - ised a friend with us to stay.
and, by Je - sus' power, he helps and saves.
when our crit - ics scorn Christ's cho - sen way.
when the Sav - iour's will we seek to know.
meant for hu - man - kind, from God a - bove.
bring - ing ev - ery bap - tised soul new birth.
you, with them, we praise, for - ev - er one.

COME, GUIDE ON EARTH OUR SPIR - IT - FRIEND; COME

TO IN - SPIRE, DI - RECT AND DE - FEND.

This is another of the melodies from Northern Ghana collected, by Tom Colvin, from the singing of people at village ceilidhs (concerts). Tom Colvin wrote these words to the melody for the new Church at Nyohene, Ghana.

This lovely song both re–tells the promise of Christ, and invokes the Spirit. It has been slightly amended in rhythm and has been harmonised. Little has been altered in the original text. However, if people feel uncomfortable with "master Jesus," it is easy to substitute "saviour Jesus." And if people are reticent to call the Spirit "he" it is quite acceptable to change that to "she." In different languages the Spirit is given different genders, and in some African tongues, the same word is used for "he" and "she." Verses may be omitted ad lib.

Other songs from Africa, collected by Tom Colvin, are found in *FILL US WITH YOUR LOVE*, published in 1983 by Agape, Illinois.

Holy forever

Tune: COLBOOTH (JLB)

Brightly

1. Ho - ly for - ev - er and ev - er is God,
2. Praise to our Mak - er and Mov - er we sing,
3. Wor - thy are you who, by shed - ding your blood,
4. Wor - thy the Lamb who was sen - tenced and slain!
5. Bless - ing and hon - our and glo - ry and might

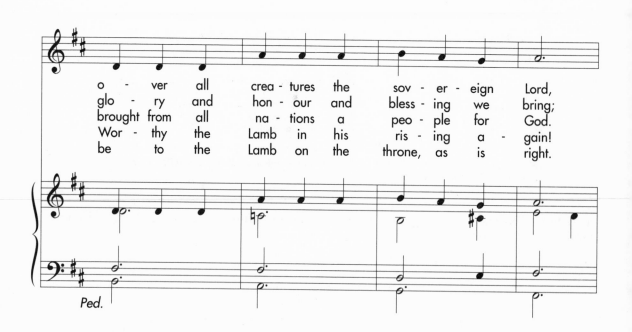

o - ver all crea - tures the sov - er - eign Lord,
glo - ry and hon - our and bless - ing we bring;
brought from all na - tions a peo - ple for God.
Wor - thy the Lamb in his ris - ing a - gain!
be to the Lamb on the throne, as is right.

Ped.

who was, and is, and who is yet to come. Al - le - lu -
all our ex - is - tence de - pends on the Lord. Al - le - lu -
Folk of all rac - es you call to be priests. Al - le - lu -
Wor - thy of pow - er and wis - dom and wealth, Al - le - lu -
Let earth and heav - en u - nite to ex - claim Al - le - lu -

Last time

ia!
ia!
ia!
ia!
ia!

A - men.

In the Book of Revelation, we are given an insight into the worship of heaven in which Christ shares since, after his ascension, he is seated at God's right hand.

This paraphrase of words from chapter five should be sung in unison and with organ accompaniment.

About the Iona Community

The Iona Community is an ecumenical community of men and women founded in Scotland in 1938—during the depths of the Great Depression and amid prospects of war. The founder, George MacLeod, was an inner city minister appalled by the lack of impact the church had on the lives of those most hard-hit by economic and political events.

MacLeod believed that ministers would understand little of working people until the ways of training clergy were changed. So in 1938, he set off to the remote island of Iona with a half-dozen young clergy and a half-dozen craftsmen to rebuild a 1,000-year-old historic abbey that had fallen into disuse. This effort would serve as a tangible sign of the unity of worship and work, church and industry, spiritual and material. Craftsmen and clergy worked as one to create what is now called the Iona Community. As a vital part of their work—and as the community grew—its members returned to the inner city to build housing and to experiment with different patterns of Christian life. The main tenets of the community became peace and justice, work and a new economic order, and community and celebration.

Today, the community is led by 200 men and women who reside mainly in Britain, but also in Africa, Australia, India, and North America. Although the community comes under the auspices of the Church of Scotland, its members are drawn from many Christian denominations, Protestant and Roman Catholic. And as with the community of Taizé, thousands journey to Iona every year for spiritual growth.

For more information about the Iona Community, write to the following address:

Iona Community
Community House
Pearce Institute
840 Govan Road
Glasgow G51 3UU
SCOTLAND

INDEX OF TITLES AND FIRST LINES*

*Italics denote first lines.